FRANCES R. CURCIO & MYRA ZARNOWSKI

THE CASE OF
ANTONIO MEUCCI
& THE TELEPHONE

—— JUST THE FACTS ——

ideapress

THE CASE OF
ANTONIO MEUCCI
& THE TELEPHONE

— JUST THE FACTS —

Author: Frances R. Curcio & Myra Zarnowski
Copy Editor: Tiziano Thomas Dossena
Editor: Leonardo Campanile
On the cover: *Antonio Meucci* by William John Castello
Cover Design and Interior Layout: Dominic A. Campanile

Images & Artwork provided by:
Garibaldi-Meucci Museum, Staten Island, NY & William John Castello

ISBN: 978-1-948651-72-1
Library of Congress Control Number: 2025919036
Published by: Idea Press *(an imprint of Idea Graphics, LLC)* — Florida, USA
www.ideapress-usa.com
Administrative Office, Florida, USA • email: ideapress33@gmail.com
Editorial Office, New York, USA • editoreusa@gmail.com

Printed in the USA - 1st Edition, September 2025

FRANCES R. CURCIO & MYRA ZARNOWSKI

THE CASE OF
ANTONIO MEUCCI
& THE TELEPHONE

—— JUST THE FACTS ——

ideapress

The Garibaldi Meucci Museum.

INTRODUCTION

Dear Reader,

In this book, we will share an important but not well-known story. We will tell you about Antonio Meucci and how he claimed he invented the telephone. You may wonder why this matters now, but it does. New facts and evidence can sometimes show us that what we once thought was true is not accurate. We will present the facts about Antonio's inventions and raise some questions for you to think about these facts.

Historians frequently revise their understandings of the past when they find convincing evidence for rethinking what they once believed. You can do this too, and we will give you information about Antonio Meucci's life, his work, and even some of his flaws. This information may convince you that Antonio is a big part of the story of the invention of the telephone.

As you will see, Antonio wasn't perfect. You might even think he caused some of his problems, but that is also part of his story.

We begin with some information about Antonio — where he lived and when, his passion for invention, and his experiences working in Italy, Cuba, and finally, the U.S. We will present the facts about his experiments and inventions as we understand them. Then you can decide what you think and share your new knowledge with others.

Frances R. Curcio — *Myra Zarnowski*

Antonio Meucci in his later years.
(Image of the time. Courtesy Garibaldi-Meucci Museum, Staten Island, NY)

A BRIEF LOOK AT
ANTONIO MEUCCI'S
LIFE AND TIMES

Antonio was born in the early 1800s, long before the telephone was invented. What was life like at that time? Suppose you had an emergency. How would you get help? What if you wanted to share good news with friends and relatives who did not live nearby, or if you just wanted to say hello to them? Without the telephone, this would be difficult, if not impossible.

Now let's take a closer look at the world in which Antonio lived. When he was a little boy in Florence, Italy, his life was different from yours. In some ways Antonio was lucky. When he was 13 years old his father sent him to The Academy of Fine Arts, where he studied electricity, acoustics, physics, engineering, and chemistry. This was unusual because most poor boys like Antonio did not go to school. Antonio was very fortunate.

When Antonio was 16 years old and his father needed help to support the family, his father found him a job as a gatekeeper. This job was hardly a match for Antonio's intelligence or his interests.

He later found a job that better matched his interests and skills when he was hired as a young stage assistant in a theater. With experience, he advanced to chief engineer in the famous Teatro della Pergola, a theater still famous today in Florence. Antonio needed to give directions from the theater's control room to the workers on the stage. Since he didn't want to run from place to place, he created an intercom system. This was the ancestor, or the beginning, of today's telephone. This made it possible to speak to the workers from a distance. It was the beginning of a long process of invention, and even Antonio didn't know where it would lead. It was also here, in Florence, Italy, where he met his future wife, Esterre.

Antonio's time in Florence came to an abrupt end when his political views and actions landed him in jail — not just once — but several times. To avoid this dangerous situation, he and his wife fled to Havana, Cuba, with a group of theater people. He became the chief engineer at the Gran Teatro de Tacón, where he continued to build his reputation for solving problems.

In 1850, after successfully living in Cuba for fifteen years, Antonio and his wife decided to leave when the Teatro de Tacón burnt down. They emigrated to New York City and settled on Staten Island, where he continued developing original and practical ideas.

In what follows in this book, we share ten facts for you to consider. After you have read these facts and our explanations, you can decide what you think about Meucci and the invention of the telephone.

FACT #1

ANTONIO HAD AN INVENTIVE MIND

Antonio was always thinking about how to solve practical problems. It was a big part of his life. When he noticed or was told about a problem, he worked on finding ways to fix it. Long before the invention of the telephone, he would work day and night in his laboratory. He was full of new and creative ideas to improve daily life.

Wherever he worked—Florence, Italy; Havana, Cuba; or Staten Island, New York—he was inventing. In 1834, he was hired as a mechanic at the Pergola Theater in Florence, where he improved the lighting in the theater and created new ways to change the stage sets rapidly. He also designed an early version of an intercom. This device was then used by the stagehands to speak with each other from a distance while changing the sets.

Later, in 1835, when he worked in the Tacón Theater in Havana, Cuba, Antonio continued to create new mechanical devices for changing sets. At this time, he also became fascinated with electricity and began considering its possible uses.

In 1850, he and his wife moved to the United States and lived on Staten Island, New York. He opened a candle factory and invented a mold to make paraffin candles. He also invented a way to use vegetable fiber for making paper. He was granted patents from the U.S. government for these inventions, which means he had the sole right to make, use, and sell them.

During this time, he remained very, very interested in how sound could travel through a copper wire and thought about it most of the time. Antonio's ability to imagine and develop new solutions to pressing problems eventually led to other inventions.

"Speaking Tubes" intercom system used at Teatro Pergola.
(Image of the time. Courtesy Garibaldi-Meucci Museum, Staten Island, NY)

THINK ABOUT IT:

In what ways did Antonio show he had the mind of an inventor?

FACT #2

ANTONIO HAD A "SPARK" OF AN IDEA

Something extraordinary happened one day in 1849 when Antonio discovered that sound could travel through a copper wire. Try to picture it: Antonio was in his lab when a man suffering from a terrible headache arrived at his house seeking help to relieve his pain. What was the treatment? It was a mild electric shock. Antonio had read that electricity could be used to cure pain and he put this knowledge to work on several patients.

When he treated patients, Antonio usually took them to his lab, but this time he left the patient in the parlor and prepared his treatment two rooms away, in his laboratory. He had the patient hold on to two insulated copper wires with a metal plate attached to each end. At the same time, he attached the other ends of the wires to a battery. And what do you think happened? The man received a shock, let out a scream, and — Are you ready? — Antonio heard the scream *not* from two rooms away, but from the wire itself. This was truly amazing! This event sparked Antonio's thinking. He thought about what he experienced, and how he might use it.

During the next thirty years, Antonio continued investigating how sound could travel through a wire. First, he made sure that the patient would not receive a shock by coating the copper plate that went in the patient's mouth with a type of cardboard. Second, he developed an earpiece and a mouthpiece that enabled listening and talking. Third, he experimented with using a horseshoe magnet to generate electricity and animal membranes that vibrate to make the voice louder. Why is this long period of development so important? It was during this time that Antonio continued to make improvements.

As you probably know, Alexander Graham Bell has been called the inventor of the telephone. So, what was he doing in 1849? Not much inventing, since he was only two years old and probably still in diapers when Antonio first discovered that sound could travel through a wire.

6

Meucci heard the scream not from
two rooms away, but from the wire itself...
(Images by William Castello)

THINK ABOUT IT:

If you are devoted to something (for example, dancing, baseball, computer games, solving puzzles, drawing), you understand what it means. You spend all your free time doing that activity. That is what Antonio did. He devoted as much time as he could to this discovery, making new models, testing them, and making improvements. He saw its possible use as a way of speaking to people who were a distance away. Since he spent so much of his time creating and refining a way to communicate from one place to another using an electric wire, should he, then, be considered the inventor of the telephone?

FACT #3

ANTONIO HAD STRENGTHS AND LIMITATIONS

Antonio had many strengths that made him a productive inventor. He could focus on solving a problem or completing a task for long periods of time, not just for weeks, but for years. As we mentioned, he worked on perfecting this invention, which he called "the speaking telegraph," for thirty years. Now that's being persistent!

In addition, he had a strong moral character. He was honest, hardworking, generous, and loyal. He was a good friend. When the Italian general Giuseppe Garibaldi was looking for a quiet place to stay, Antonio welcomed him into his home on Staten Island and provided him with employment in his candle factory.

As a caring husband, Antonio was devoted to his wife. When she was ill, she was confined to her bed on the second floor of their house. When she needed something, he set up a way to communicate with her from his laboratory. This turned out to be the first functioning telephone.

However, he also had serious shortcomings. First, Antonio's knowledge of English was limited, and yet he made no effort to learn the language. When he was living and working in Havana, Cuba, the Spanish-speaking people could understand his use of Italian. In New York, his limited English became a problem in a number of situations. He couldn't explain his ideas clearly or read important documents. He couldn't write directions for creating and using his inventions. Without an interpreter, he couldn't defend himself in a discussion or argument.

Second, Antonio avoided his responsibilities. Like most adults, Antonio had responsibilities, such as earning money to support himself and his wife and effectively running his business. He owned a candle factory, but instead of watching over it and supervising its production of candles, he spent many hours working in his laboratory. He even left the running of the factory to others, who were not reliable at best or who cheated him at worst.

Third, William Rider, a shrewd and dishonest businessman, was able to take advantage of Antonio's poor English skills and his lack of interest in business details. When he saw the value of Antonio's ideas for candle-making, Rider started a candle-making factory with Antonio. He even took over the patent rights of some of Antonio's inventions. The company was a success, but Rider kept the profits for himself. When the factory burnt down, Rider collected the insurance money and again did not share the money fairly with Antonio.

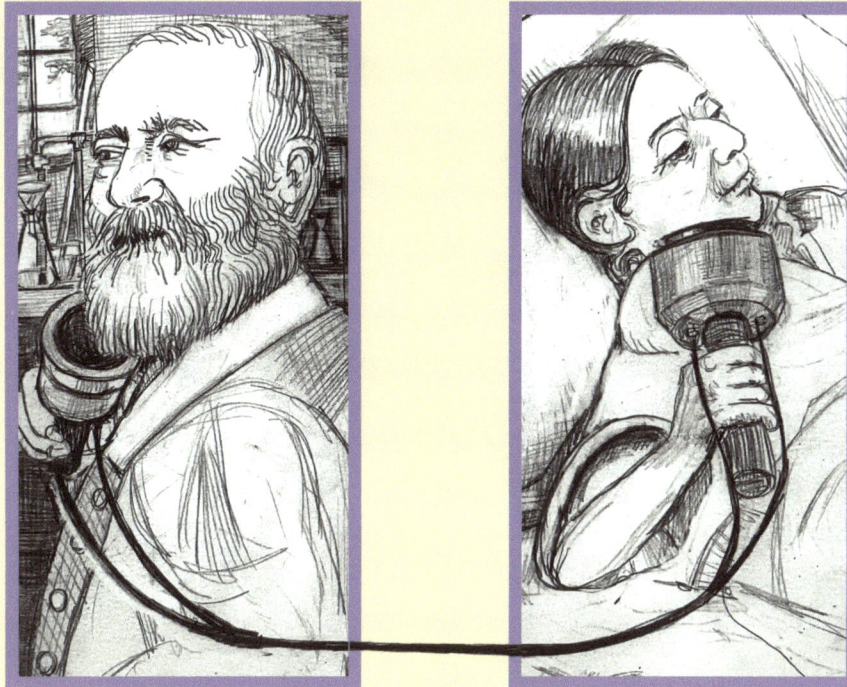

Antonio in Lab, Esterre in bed, talking on telettrofono.
(Images by William Castello)

THINK ABOUT IT:

Why didn't Antonio watch his business more carefully? Perhaps he had no interest. Or he couldn't understand the business documents (orders, sales, profits, bills, contracts) because they were in English. Were these good excuses? What do you think?

FACT #4

ANTONIO SUFFERED SERIOUS INJURIES AND HIS TELEPHONE MODELS WERE SOLD TO COVER THE BILLS

Sometimes, in life, something unexpected occurs, preventing us from following through with our plans. This is called a setback, and that's what happened to Antonio. He wanted to spend time improving his invention and getting a patent for it, a document that would prove that it was his idea. Instead, Antonio had a terrible accident and landed in the hospital for several months.

Here's what happened. On July 30, 1871, Antonio was a passenger on the ferryboat Westfield when the boiler exploded. The steam explosion killed more than 100 passengers and landed Antonio in the hospital for several months with severe burns all over his body. To make matters worse, Antonio's wife was not only ill and confined to her bed, she was also extremely poor. That's why she sold all his models and equipment for a meager $6, or about $150 in today's currency. These were all the things he needed to get the patent for his telephone.

While someone else might have given up, not Antonio! Even though this was an enormous setback, Antonio kept on working on his invention and taking steps to recreate his work.

Westfield steamboat explosion.
• Harper's Magazine, Saturday, 12 August 1871 issue, Volume XV, No. 763, page 1. •
(Sketched from the Hurricane Deck of the "Northfield" by W. Long Palin)

THINK ABOUT IT:

Was Antonio responsible for his setback? What if Antonio had not taken the ferryboat that exploded? How might getting a patent for his invention have been different?

FACT #5

ANTONIO FILED TEMPORARY CLAIMS TO HIS INVENTION IN 1871, 1872, AND 1873

Once Antonio recovered from his injuries, he took steps to claim ownership of his invention. He could not afford the $250 cost of a patent ($6,286 in 2024 dollars) that would give him legal ownership of his invention. His lawyer suggested that he apply for a temporary claim called a *caveat*. In 1871, with the help of his friends, he paid $20, $10 for the lawyer, and $10 for the caveat ($252 for each in 2024 dollars). This document would now prove and protect the ownership of his idea for one year. He then renewed it in 1872 and 1873.

Unfortunately, the caveat did not provide enough protection for his idea. Here's why. It did not adequately describe his invention because his translator and lawyer did not understand the details of the invention. The original caveat prepared by the lawyer left out essential information. When Antonio reviewed it with the help of his friend who served as his interpreter, he added the important details. Unfortunately, the lawyer did not understand the importance of these details, so he erased them. This meant the caveat was weak. After the third caveat expired, Antonio could no longer afford to renew it. He lost the protection he once had.

In the future, this lack of legal protection would cause devastating results: In 1876, Alexander Graham Bell was granted a patent for the telephone and became very wealthy, while Antonio was shockingly poor.

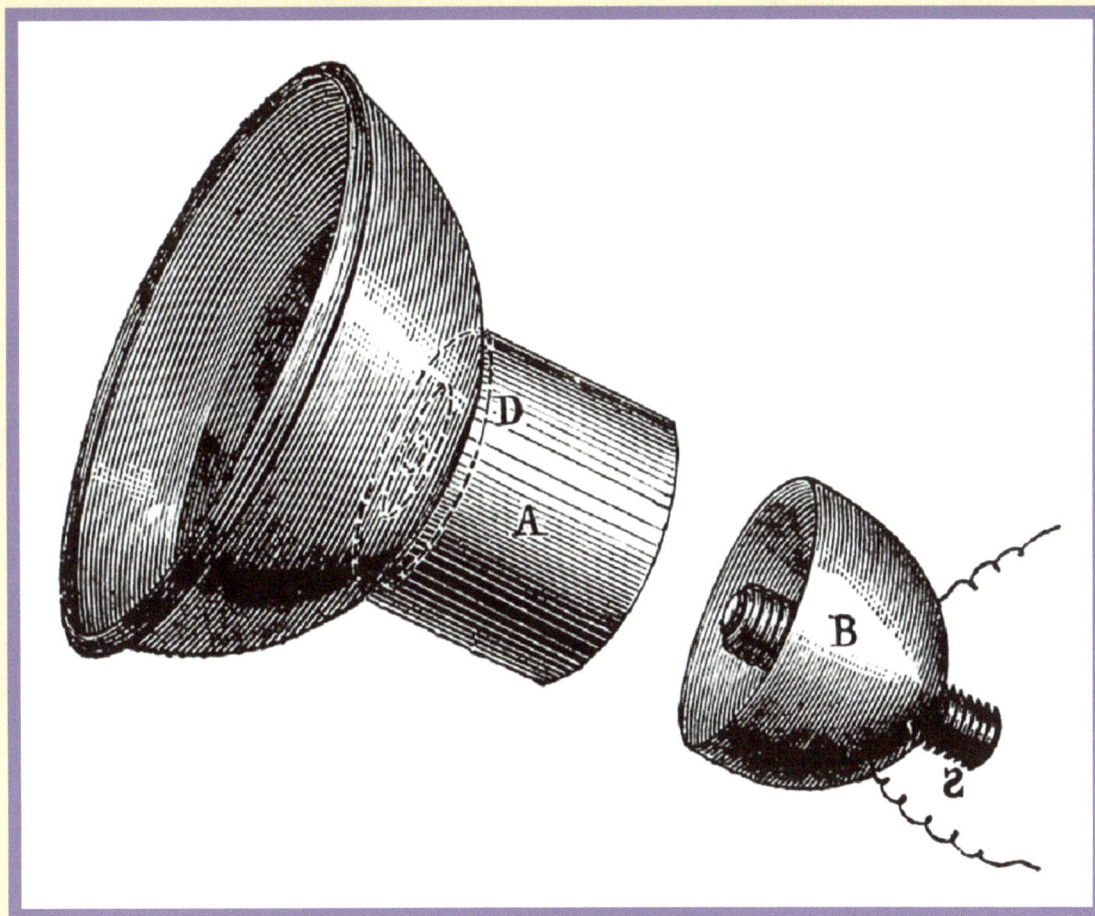

Graphic view of the Meucci telephone transmitter.
(Image of the time. Courtesy Garibaldi-Meucci Museum, Staten Island, NY)

THINK ABOUT IT:

Did this have to happen? Was it fair? Was it right?
Was there anything Antonio could have done to keep the ownership of his ideas?

FACT #6

ANTONIO'S DOCUMENTS "DISAPPEARED"

Several months after Antonio recovered from the ferry boat accident, he was desperate to find a way to test his recreated sound telegraph, the *telettrofono*. His attempt was a disaster. Here's what happened. One of Antonio's friends took him to the American District Telegraph Company, a part of Western Union, where he met with the vice president, Mr. Grant. Antonio wanted to test his talking telegraph over the Western Union wires. Although Mr. Grant laughed at Antonio's idea, he agreed to a test at a future time. Trusting Mr. Grant, Antonio left all of his papers describing his invention and a sample model with him. Mr. Grant then gave everything to Mr. Durant, an assistant, who put the papers in his drawer. Many months passed as Antonio tried to set up an appointment to test his invention, but he was ignored. Not fully understanding the papers, Mr. Durant gave them back to Mr. Grant. Antonio did not give up. He sent his friend to get all his materials, but his friend was told that they were "missing."

This was devastating news! But there is even more. The papers changed hands once more when they were given to two technicians who placed the material in the laboratory at Western Union. It was in this very laboratory that two scientists, Elisha Gray and Alexander Graham Bell were working on a way to transmit musical sounds through a single wire. Then, a startling thing happened. In 1876, at almost exactly the same time, both Gray and Bell announced that they had invented the telephone! Bell filed for a patent, and two hours after that Gray filed for a caveat. Their descriptions of their inventions were *similar* to Antonio's. To make matters worse, the file with Antonio's earlier caveats had disappeared from the Patent Office, with only the caveat number still remaining.

Alexander Graham Bell holding "Patent."
(Image by William Castello)

What could have happened to Antonio's papers and his model?
Was it a coincidence that the two scientists claimed to invent the telephone and
request ownership of the idea at just about the same time?
Was it a coincidence that their descriptions closely resembled Antonio's?

15

FACT #7

ANTONIO AND BELL WENT TO COURT

Antonio was losing more and more control of his invention to Alexander Graham Bell, and in the end, their dispute landed in court. It started after Alexander Graham Bell filed for and was granted a patent for the telephone. He then began to exhibit and demonstrate what he referred to as *his* invention. Bell displayed his telephone at the Centennial Exposition in Philadelphia in 1876. It was a celebration of America's 100th anniversary of independence. The emperor of Brazil, Pedro II, stopped at Bell's exhibit, and he was the first person to try the new device, enthusiastically declaring, "My God! It talks!"

Newspapers across the country reported this exciting story. When one of Antonio's friends sent him a newspaper article describing this incident, Antonio became enraged because Bell was taking credit for his invention. A friend helped Antonio write letters to the newspapers explaining that his idea had been robbed. Antonio was angry and tried to have these errors corrected. To make matters worse, in 1877, Bell and his associates founded the Bell Telephone Company, and in 1879, Western Union recognized Bell as the inventor of the telephone. Antonio's work of over thirty years was slipping away from him.

Yet, there was also growing support for Antonio. In 1883, Antonio signed an agreement giving the Globe Telephone Company the rights to his invention of the telephone. The company then began collecting all of Antonio's writings, documents, and drawings, proving that he was the actual inventor of the telephone. They also gathered statements from people who had seen or used Antonio's telephone. The company accused Bell of fraud, or cheating, claiming that his patent was a corrupt use of Antonio's design. In 1885, the Globe Telephone Company sued Bell. The Bell Telephone Company, in turn, then sued the Globe Telephone Company for infringing, or violating their patent for the telephone. The battle to determine the true inventor of the telephone began.

Antonio Meucci and his telettrofono.
(Image by William Castello)

Whose case is the stronger, Bell's or Antonio's?
Who has a better chance of winning in court? Why?

FACT #8

ANTONIO LOST THE COURT CASE TO ALEXANDER GRAHAM BELL

How was it possible that Antonio lost the case? After all, he had worked on his invention for over thirty years, adding many, many improvements. He had demonstrated his telephone to a number of people, who testified in court that they used the invention in his house. Antonio also kept extensive notes and journals describing his work. So, what happened? Why did Antonio lose to Bell? Here are some possible reasons:

- Antonio couldn't speak English well, so during the trial he relied on an interpreter to translate questions to him in Italian and then translate his answers from Italian to English. This caused problems because the interpreter was not familiar with the technical vocabulary Antonio used, so the translations were often incorrect or confusing. Even though Antonio spoke at length, he was misunderstood.

- While many people testified that they had seen or used Antonio's invention in his house long before Bell filed his patent, they did not convince the judge. Almost fifty people made sworn declarations or testified in court for Antonio. John Fleming, the junk dealer, swore that he bought the material Antonio used for his invention from Antonio's wife in 1871, well before Bell filed his patent in 1876. The painter, Nestore Corradi, testified that he created a drawing showing two people using Antonio's invention to communicate. This drawing was filed along with Antonio's application for a caveat to prove he was the inventor of the telephone. Matilda Ciuci, a woman who lived with the Meuccis and assisted Antonio's wife Esterre, declared that she helped Antonio by trying out his invention in several locations in and around his house. Even though many people spoke up for Antonio, the judge did not find their arguments convincing. Why? Was he prejudiced against Italian immigrants and unwilling to take their evidence seriously? Was he unwilling to decide against the wealthy and powerful Bell Telephone Company? Or did he honestly believe the evidence was false?

- The whole file of documents containing Antonio's caveat and description of his invention was missing from the Patent Office. Since the caveat, drawings, and documents Antonio had submitted were missing when the case went to trial, he and his attorney could not refer to these materials. What might have happened to them?
- The Bell Telephone Company had become very wealthy since its founding in 1876. They could afford a high-priced, well-respected lawyer to help them win their case. That lawyer, James Jackson Storrow, had extensive knowledge of electricity and mechanics as well as being a competent lawyer. He brought in many experts to testify that Antonio's caveat did not describe Bell's patented invention. One such expert, Robert Cross, was a professor of physics and a friend of Bell; he described Antonio's invention as a mere "string toy." He even claimed it was copied from Bell. Judge William James Wallace accepted these arguments. Why?

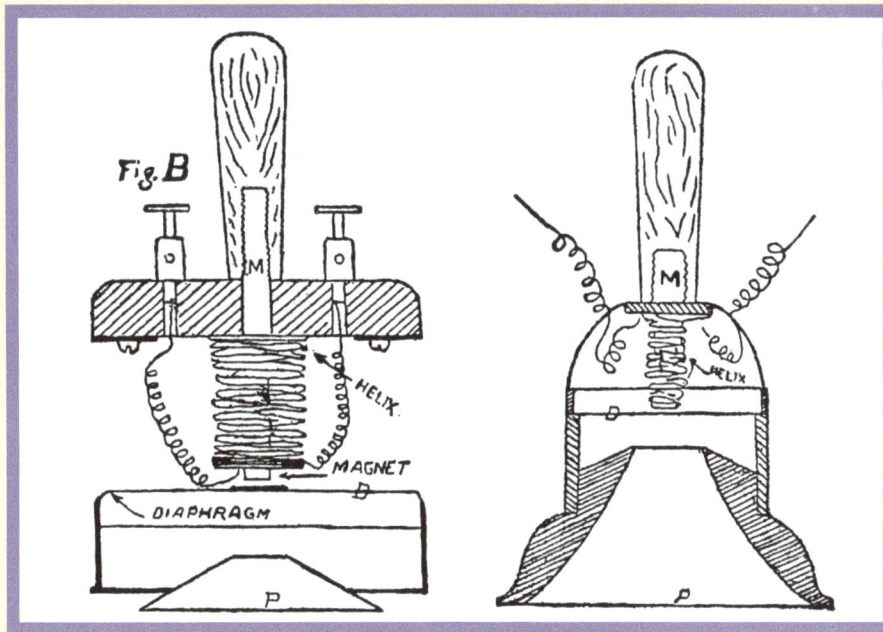

Meucci's telephone caveat drawing.
(Courtesy Garibaldi-Meucci Museum, Staten Island, NY)

THINK ABOUT IT:

Was it right that Bell won the case and Antonio lost? Was it fair? Why?

FACT #9

ANTONIO IS ACKNOWLEDGED AS THE TRUE INVENTOR OF THE TELEPHONE BY A U.S. CONGRESSIONAL RESOLUTION

Not everyone has accepted Bell's triumph over Meucci. In 2002, one hundred thirteen years after Antonio's death, Staten Island Congressman Vito Fossella successfully sponsored a Congressional Resolution, referred to as H. R. 269, acknowledging Antonio as the *true* inventor of the telephone.

Now that you have read facts 1-8, you are already familiar with much of the content of the Congressional Resolution. They include Antonio's surprising discovery that sound can travel through a wire, the 30 years he spent improving his "talking telegraph," and the many witnesses who observed his use of the telephone to communicate with his invalid wife. Antonio's inability to speak English interfered with his ability to communicate, clarify, and justify his ideas. Therefore, to correct the miscarriage of justice, a re-examination of the evidence led to this Congressional Resolution:

"It is the sense of the House of Representatives that the life and achievements of Antonio Meucci should be recognized, and his work in the invention of the telephone should be acknowledged."

At the end of his life, Antonio had lost everything — his wife, his home, the court case, and his money. But he still had his friends and supporters and those devoted to helping him and bringing justice, even after his death.

H. Res. 269
In the House of Representatives, U.S.,
June 11, 2002.

Whereas Antonio Meucci, the great Italian inventor, had a career that was both extraordinary and tragic;

Whereas, upon immigrating to New York, Meucci continued to work with ceaseless vigor on a project he had begun in Havana, Cuba, an invention he later called the "teletrofono", involving electronic communications;

Whereas Meucci set up a rudimentary communications link in his Staten Island home that connected the basement with the first floor, and later, when his wife began to suffer from crippling arthritis, he created a permanent link between his lab and his wife's second floor bedroom;

Whereas, having exhausted most of his life's savings in pursuing his work, Meucci was unable to commercialize his invention, though he demonstrated his invention in 1860 and had a description of it published in New York's Italian language newspaper;

Whereas Meucci never learned English well enough to navigate the complex American business community;

Whereas Meucci was unable to raise sufficient funds to pay his way through the patent application process, and thus had to settle for a caveat, a one year renewable notice of an impending patent, which was first filed on December 28, 1871;

Whereas Meucci later learned that the Western Union affiliate laboratory reportedly lost his working models, and Meucci, who at this point was living on public assistance, was unable to renew the caveat after 1874;

Whereas in March 1876, Alexander Graham Bell, who conducted experiments in the same laboratory where Meucci's materials had been stored, was granted a patent and was thereafter credited with inventing the telephone;

Whereas on January 13, 1887, the Government of the United States moved to annul the patent issued to Bell on the grounds of fraud and misrepresentation, a case that the Supreme Court found viable and remanded for trial;

Whereas Meucci died in October 1889, the Bell patent expired in January 1893, and the case was discontinued as moot without ever reaching the underlying issue of the true inventor of the telephone entitled to the patent; and

Whereas if Meucci had been able to pay the $10 fee to maintain the caveat after 1874, no patent could have been issued to Bell: Now, therefore, be it

Resolved, That it is the sense of the House of Representatives that the life and achievements of Antonio Meucci should be recognized, and his work in the invention of the telephone should be acknowledged.

THINK ABOUT IT:

Why do you think it took 113 years after Antonio died for the U.S. House of Representatives to recognize his achievement? What else could be done to recognize Antonio's invention?

FACT #10

ANTONIO'S HOUSE IS NOW A MUSEUM THAT CELEBRATES HIS LIFE AND WORK

Owned by the Order of the Sons and Daughters of Italy in America, the Garibaldi-Meucci Museum opened to the public in 1956. It is dedicated to the memory of Italian general Giuseppe Garibaldi and inventor Antonio Meucci. If you want to know more about Antonio Meucci's life and work, you can visit this museum on Staten Island, or you can visit it online at www.garibaldimeuccimuseum.com.

What's in the museum? How does it celebrate Antonio's life and work? If you visited the museum, you could see a sample of his telephone with its receiver and speaker, a chair and piano he constructed, and many photographs, documents, and newspaper articles about Antonio. There are exhibits, classes, lectures, and competitions for students to enter.

Meucci and other people on the porch of his house in 1886. The house at the time was named "Garibaldi Homestead" since the Italian Hero had resided in it for a few months as a guest of Meucci.
(Image of the time. Courtesy Garibaldi-Meucci Museum, Staten Island, NY)

THINK ABOUT IT:

What would you like to see in the museum that would
help you better understand Antonio's life and work?

A NOTE FROM THE AUTHORS
FRAN AND MYRA

We became interested in learning more about Antonio Meucci in different ways. Fran, who is Italian American, has always been interested in her Italian heritage, and one result of this interest is that she became involved with the Garibaldi-Meucci Museum on Staten Island, New York. When she learned that there was interest in having a children's book about Meucci at the museum, she decided to write one. She asked Myra, who is interested in children's literature and history, to work with her. Together, we had a good time figuring out how to do this. It was not easy, but it was enjoyable, and we both learned heaps of new information that we put together for you.

We wanted to give you, the reader, the experience of deciding who you think invented the telephone. Using the facts and thought questions, what is your conclusion? Was it Bell or Meucci? Remember, *invention* means developing something new, something no one else thought of before. What evidence convinced you? You should have several reasons, not just one or two. Remember, understanding what happened in the past is about using evidence to shape your ideas. It's like solving a puzzle. We hope you enjoyed coming to your own conclusion.

Marianna Randazzo is gratefully recognized for motivating the development of this book and providing resources to support the facts.

We also wish to thank two young readers, Corbin and Zachary, who provided their reactions to the content and clarity of our telling of Antonio's story.

Frances R. Curcio - Myra Zarnowski

FRANCES R. CURCIO

Frances R. Curcio is Professor Emerita at Queens College of the City University of New York, where she taught the history and philosophy of education and methods of teaching mathematics. Interest in her Italian/American roots led to extensive research and the publication of *Mio Nonno Totore and the American Dream* (Idea Press, 2024).

MYRA ZARNOWSKI

Myra Zarnowski is Professor Emerita at Queens College of the City University of New York, where she taught courses in social studies, children's literature, and literacy. She is interested in helping children use historical evidence to interpret the past.

WILLIAM JOHN CASTELLO

William John Castello is an Adjunct Professor of Communications at St. John's University and was a Graphic Journalist at the Associated Press for thirty-five years. He is currently the artist-in-residence and contributor to the Garibaldi-Meucci Museum.

Workers inside the Meucci candle factory with Giuseppe Garibaldi.
(Courtesy Garibaldi-Meucci Museum, Staten Island, NY)

Bibliography

- Catania, Basilio. "Antonio Meucci: Telephone Pioneer." *Bulletin of Science, Technology & Society* 21 no. 1 (February 2001): 55-76.
- _____. "The U. S. Government versus Alexander Graham Bell: An Important Acknowledgement for Antonio Meucci." *Bulletin of Science, Technology and Society* - 22 no. 6 (December 2002): 426-442.
- _____. "Historian's Corner—Antonio Meucci: How Electrotherapy Gave Birth to Telephony." *European Transactions on Telecommunications* 14 (January 2004): 539-552.
- _____. *Antonio Meucci: The Inventor and His Times, Part 1: From Florence to Havana.* Italia: SEAT, Divisione STET s.p.a., 1994, 1999.
- _____. *Antonio Meucci: The Inventor and His Times, Part II: New York, 1850-1871.* Italia: SEAT, Divisione STET s.p.a., 1994, 1999.
- House of Representatives of the United States Congress. (2001, 17 October-2002, 11 June). House Resolution No. 269, of the 107th Congress, 1st Session. https://www.govinfo.gov/content/pkg/BILLS-107hres269ih/pdf/BILLS-107hres269ih.pdf
- Chaparro, Laura. "Antonio Meucci, the Italian Immigrant Who Couldn't Patent the Telephone." *Open Mind*, October 18, 2017. https://www.bbvaopenmind.com/en/science/leading-figures/antonio-meucci-the-italian-immigrant-who-couldnt-patent-the-telephone/
- "Meucci's Claims to the Telephone—With Description of His Instrument and 10 Figures." *Scientific American Supplement XX*, no. 520 Supp (December 19, 1885): 8304-8305. https://babel.hathitrust.org/cgi/pt?id=rul.39030032845937&seq=407
- Nese, Marco, and Francesco Nicotra. *Antonio Meucci.* Roma, Italia: Editrice Italy Publisher, 1989.
- Schiavo, Giovanni E. *Antonio Meucci Inventor of the Telephone.* NYC: The Vigo Press, 1958.

Filmography

- DeNonno, Tony. *Antonio Meucci: The Father of the Telephone*, n.d. (A film by Tony DeNonno.) https://www.denonnoprodinc.com (Italian American Film Series.)
- Evangelista, Anton. *ANTONIO MEUCCI: The Original Inventor of the Telephone.* Staten Island, NY: Garibaldi-Meucci Museum, n.d. (A film by Anton Evangelista). https://www.youtube.com/watch?v=EBnQ4sKMnb4

Children's Book

- Schwartz, Ella. *Stolen Science.* New York: Bloomsbury Children's Books, 2021.

www.ingramcontent.com/pod-product-compliance
Lightning Source LLC
LaVergne TN
LVHW072059070426
835508LV00002B/184